Rules
for
School

BY ALEC GREVEN

ILLUSTRATIONS BY KEI ACEDERA

Collins

An Imprint of HarperCollins*Publishers*

This book is for people who work in schools
and make it an awesome place to be.

Collins is an imprint of HarperCollins Publishers.

Rules for School
Text copyright © 2010 by Alec Greven
Illustrations copyright © 2010 by Kei Acedera
All rights reserved.

Printed in the United States of America.

Library of Congress Cataloging-in-Publication Data
Greven, Alec.
  Rules for school / by Alec Greven ; illustrations by Kei Acedera. — 1st ed.
    p. cm.
  ISBN 978-0-06-195170-1 (trade bdg.)
  1. Elementary schools—Juvenile literature. 2. School children—Juvenile literature. 3. School day—Juvenile literature. I. Acedera, Kei, ill. II. Title.
LB1556.G74 2010   2010008138
372.18—dc22   CIP
                                                                                          AC

Typography by Ray Shappell

10 11 12 13 14 LP/WOR 10 9 8 7 6 5 4 3 2 1

❖ First Edition

Do you have a teacher or
someone else at school
who is special to you?
Tell them! Say thank you.

This book is for

_____

from

_____

INTRODUCTION

I have gone to school for a few years now, so I have a lot of experience in this area. I'm going to share my tips to help you get ready, take charge, and rule the school.

Kids have a lot of questions about school. What if you get lost? Will your teacher be nice? Who will you eat lunch with and play with at recess?

I love everything about school: the subjects, the activities, the teachers, the library—everything. But there are some things that are tough, like doing your homework and knowing where to sit in the cafeteria.

You might love school or hate it, but you have to go, so just make the best of it.

Here are your rules for school success. Have fun!

Rule 1: You have to let go of summer.

It is hard to believe that summer is over. But it is. It's time to get down to business.

This means getting ready in your mind. This is difficult but *very* important. First you have to let go of summer. This means letting campouts, staying up late, swimming, and playing outside wash out of your mind.

It's a good idea to switch to "school time" three days before the first day of school. It is like a time change when you travel. This helps kids avoid shock and trauma on the first day of school.

Rule 2: Gear up and get that backpack ready!

Before you start school, you need to get all your new school things like supplies, clothes, backpack, and lunch box. This is the easy part.

Rule 3: You're going to be nervous—get over it.

The first day of school is scary and exciting.

Ask if you can meet your teacher and see your classroom before the first day. Most teachers are nice, so don't worry too much. Explore the school a little bit so you know how to get around.

FACT: 21% of kids are excited to go to school, 70% of kids are scared, and 9% of kids just don't really care.

Rule 4: Get Mom on your side.

On the first day of school, your mom usually makes you wear something fancy. Don't let the pressure get to you. Try to convince her to let you wear something else so you don't stick out from the crowd.

Another day that your mom might make you dress up is on school picture day. Don't fight her on this one. She thinks it will make you look good in your photo, but it doesn't help. The photographer usually makes you sit in a weird pose with your head tilted and then asks you to say something like "cheeseburger." Then he takes the picture while you are talking, so your mouth looks funny.

You are very lucky if your school pictures come out decent. But even if they aren't good, your parents will still buy them. This will be embarrassing down the road. Trust me.

Rule 5: Stay on track!

It's hard to get going in the morning, but try to get a routine down. If you are always forgetting to brush your teeth, make your bed, and pack your lunch box, your parents will get bossy, crazy, and agitated.

You have to stay away from distractions like video games or you are doomed!

Rule 6: Think before you sit.

It's exciting to walk into school on the first day! Sometimes you have your name on your desk and sometimes you get to pick where to sit.

If you get to pick, choosing your seat is important—it's strategy time. If you sit in the front, you have to be extra good because the teacher can see you. This is too risky. If you sit in the back, you can goof off, but that can backfire. The middle is the safe zone . . . like a neutral country.

Quiet kids are safer to sit next to. If you sit next to your friends during class, then you will probably get in trouble for talking and acting up. It's too much temptation. The cafeteria is a free zone, so wait until lunch to go crazy and talk as much as you want.

Rule 7: Be brave—ask questions!

At first the school might seem big and you won't know where everything is, like the bathroom, and how to get a hall pass if you need to go. You could just wander around, but that could take all day and you don't want to end up in the teachers' lounge by mistake. So don't be shy. Ask questions.

It might take time to learn where everything is, but soon you will rule the school and be the expert. You'll be cruising the halls with confidence. Then it is your turn to help the new kids!

Rule 8: Avoid the supernova.

Most kids are going to get in trouble at some point during class. There are three levels of punishment you need to know about:

✓ **Warning**

For little things, like talking when you are not supposed to, you might have your name written on the board. This is only a warning. Code Yellow.

✓ **Trouble**

For bigger things, like not doing your homework, you could lose a recess. Code Orange.

✓ **Supernova**

For really bad things, like fighting at school, you might have to see the principal. Beware, this is the supernova. Code Red.

Don't worry about getting in trouble once in a while. As long as you avoid the supernova, you will be fine.

There are three main things that *always* bug teachers and get you into trouble.

The **zone out** is when you are looking at your teacher but your mind is in Hawaii. If the teacher calls on you, you are busted. This is embarrassing because the teacher will give you away to the entire class, and you will have no idea what is going on.

TIP: If you attempt the zone out, come back to Earth a few times in case your teacher calls on you so maybe you can pull it off.

Interruptions and annoyances are things like tapping your pencil, humming, or playing with your scissors. This is what teachers call "disrupting the learning environment," and it really gets under their skin.

tap!
tap!

Shling!

Off task is when you are doing anything but what you are supposed to be doing, like writing a note to your friend or reading your book from home. I've done this, and let me tell you, you can't talk your way out of this. Don't even try.

Rule 9: Just face it. Homework is something you have to do.

Most kids hate homework. But not doing it will get you into major trouble.

There are three parts to doing homework:
- ✔ Bringing it home
- ✔ Doing it
- ✔ Bringing it back

Many kids forget at least one of the three parts. Doing two won't help you! You have to remember **ALL** of them.

TIP: When you forget your homework, just tell the truth.
Teachers know all the excuses, so it's no use.

Rule 10: Let loose at lunch.

Some kids worry that they won't know who to sit with at lunch.
Here's what works for me.

Size up the lunchroom. You can either sit next to people you know
or try to make new friends. Then turn on your talking switch.

One thing you can always talk about is the lunchroom food. If you're lucky, maybe it's pizza day. If it's meat loaf surprise, you're out of luck. Maybe you can make friends by trading snacks from home.

Rule 11: Run the ants out of your pants.

Recess is the time to play and get all of your energy out. This is a brain break and gives you time to run the ants out of your pants. There are lots of things to do at recess, like four square, kickball, soccer, football, monkey on the ground, slides, and swings.

Hit that blacktop and run wild!

Unfortunately, recess is an easy thing for a teacher to take away as a punishment, so be careful. If you goof off right before lunch, your recess is pretty much out of there. Beware.

FACT: A lot of kids live for recess.

Rule 12: Just be yourself.

Many kids worry about fitting in. Believe me, this happens to everyone. Be yourself. You will end up with plenty of friends by the end of the year.

Be yourself.

Here's a go-to guide of who's who in the classroom:

A **teacher's pet** is when the teacher likes you so much that you can do almost anything you want and not get in trouble. This is a safe haven, but it makes you unpopular with the other kids.

Being the **smartest kid** in the class is incredibly good as long as you are not the teacher's pet too. This position is awesome. Usually the smartest kid in the class is kind of like the deputy to the teacher.

Class clowns tell jokes and do funny things during class. This makes kids laugh, but not teachers. Class clowns get into trouble a lot.

Athletes love sports. They play, talk, and live for sports. Usually athletes aren't the best people to go to for advice (unless it is about sports) because their heads are always in the game.

Shy kids either want to be left alone or are too nervous to make friends. If you are shy, you could become friends with another shy person. This way you can relate. Or you could become friends with a talkative person. That way you could learn from them and they'll do all the talking so you won't have to!

An individual doesn't like to blend in. So they stand out. You don't have to be like everyone else. Some kids like to wear different clothes, play different games, and do the opposite of what everyone else is doing.

Everyone will meet a **bully** at some point, so you might as well be prepared. If you get confronted by a bully, don't show any signs of fear. Try to stay calm and say stop. Don't let the bully get you down.

In school there's every kind of kid. That's what makes it interesting!

Rule 13: Appreciate your teacher.

Without teachers, nothing would work and we wouldn't know anything.

Teachers help you love things even if you think you don't like them at first.

If you get lazy and do sloppy work, that tells the teacher you are not trying. Teachers don't like this. If you answer questions, even if your answers are wrong, the teacher sees you're doing your best. They love this.

If you try, you will learn 60% more things.

Sometimes your teacher can't be in class and you will have a substitute.

Some kids are not nice to subs and try to trick them. You can trick subs 72% of the time because they don't know the classroom or the rules. But it is not a very nice thing to do, and I don't recommend it. Plus, your teacher usually finds out and then you are in double trouble. Watch out.

Hello, I'm Mr. M

Rule 14: Make the most of it.

There will be things you don't want to do in school. Some days will be hard and will make you crazy.

But don't let it get to you. Overall, school is a fun place to be. Trust me.

You get to be with your friends and try all kinds of things, like band, student council, and clubs.

If you like sports, PE might be your favorite class; and if you like to talk, lunch is probably your favorite time of day. If you like to play games, recess is your thing.

My favorite time is Library because books are awesome.

TIP: If you don't like a book, don't worry. There is a book for everyone. Ask the librarian to help you.

Your parents will ask you every day after school what you learned. Most kids say "nothing" or "I don't know." But that isn't true. Maybe you learned that Andrew Jackson was the seventh president of the United States or that the playground has a secret hiding place. Tell your parents—it will make them happy.

Tip: You will learn at least one new thing at school every day. I guarantee it.

School helps you get ready for life and become independent. It isn't just about learning to read and do math. You learn to do things on your own and get along with others. Sometimes you have problems in school and have to figure them out, just like in real life.

You have to go to school, so make the most of it. Even though some things will be scary or boring, a lot of things will be exciting and interesting.

Rule 15: Have fun!